Table of
CONTENTS

D0126973

Baby owl Paul stands beside his sister, Babe. Eastern screech-owls can be red, like Paul, or gray, like Babe.

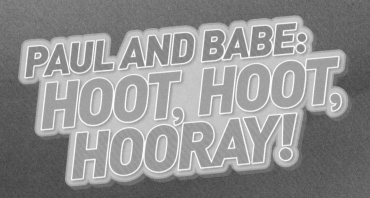

PAUL AND BABE: HOOT, HOOT, HOORAY!

When Homer Kuhn found these little baby owls, their eyes were still closed.

Chapter 1

May 1, 2013
New Creek, West Virginia, U.S.A.

It was a sunny day, without a cloud in the sky. Birds chirped, squirrels barked, hawks screamed, and a family of deer ate grass near the edge of the woods. Woodcutter Homer Kuhn (sounds like COON) had just finished sawing the base of a dried-out tree.

"Timber!" Homer called.

The tree hit the ground. *Thud!*

Homer looped a long, heavy chain around the log. His brother, Willie, pulled the log out of the forest using a large machine that looks like a tractor, called a skidder. As the log slid past Homer, a flash of white caught his eye. He thought he saw two snowballs lying on the ground. But Homer knew that they couldn't be snowballs. It was 80°F (26.5°C) outside.

Homer says, "I thought, what in the world is lying white like that in the middle of the woods?" He walked over to investigate. Lying in the dirt were two baby eastern screech-owls.

Homer scooped up the baby owls, or owlets, in his hand. They looked like two fluffy marshmallows. *Peep, peep!* the owlets called. *They must have fallen out of a hole in the log,* Homer thought.

Some birds build nests. Not screech-owls. Instead, they nest inside tree cavities (sounds like KAV-uh-tees). These are holes made by other animals, like woodpeckers. Usually, the mother owl looks after the babies while the father owl hunts for food to bring back to the family.

Homer searched the area for the owlets' parents. He looked inside the holes of other trees. But he found no parent owls. Homer knew that if he left the owlets in the woods with no home and no parents, they would die. He wrapped the babies in an old T-shirt. Then he pulled his cell phone out of his pocket and called the one person he knew would help.

"Hello," said Mrs. Tammi Kuhn.

"Hi, Mom," Homer answered. "We have something."

"Is it squirrels again?" Mrs. Kuhn asked.

"No, we found two baby owls this time," Homer said.

"Oh my!" said Mrs. Kuhn. "I'll be right there."

Mrs. Kuhn was used to getting calls like this from her sons. Homer and Willie work for a logging company. They spend most days in the woods, cutting down trees. Then they sell the logs they collect to a nearby sawmill to be cut into boards and sold as lumber. Sometimes, in the woods, the brothers find baby animals.

Owls, Owls, Everywhere

Owls live on every continent except Antarctica. They come in many shapes and sizes. The Eurasian (sounds like yur-AY-zhun) eagle-owl can grow to more than two feet (0.6 m) tall. It can weigh up to ten pounds (4.5 kg). The elf owl only grows to around six inches (15 cm) tall. It weighs less than half as much as this book. Owls' feathers help them blend into their habitats. The snowy owl's thick white feathers hide it from enemies in the frozen Arctic. And the gray- and rust-colored feathers of a screech-owl make it seem to disappear next to a tree.

Eurasian eagle-owl

"If we find baby squirrels or baby raccoons, we try to rescue them," Homer says. "We find a lot of squirrels." When the boys spot these animals, they call their mother for help. "She raises them until they are old enough to care for themselves," says Homer. Then Mrs. Kuhn returns the animals to the wild.

Mrs. Kuhn has raised and released many squirrels over the years. But screech-owls were different. She had never cared for screech-owls. In fact, it is illegal to raise them in West Virginia. But these babies needed help.

Mrs. Kuhn got in her car and drove to the edge of the woods. "I really didn't know what to do with baby screech-owls, but I didn't want them to die," says

Mrs. Kuhn. She called everyone she knew, trying to find a rescue center that could take

Did You Know?

There are more than 200 species (sounds like SPEE-sheez), or kinds, of owls.

them. Meanwhile, she drove the owlets back to her house. She put them in a box with a heating pad to keep them warm, and she did her best to feed them.

In the wild, baby screech-owls stay in the nest for about one month. Then they begin to learn how to fly and hunt. After that, the parents continue to protect and feed their young owls for two or three more months, until they can hunt on their own. But the baby owls' eyes were still closed. They were less than a week old.

Owls are carnivores (sounds like CAR-nuh-vors). They eat meat. The owlets' parents would have fed the babies insects and small mammals, like mice. All Mrs. Kuhn had was frozen hamburger and deer meat. She thawed the meat and cut it into small chunks. Then she used tweezers to feed the meat to the "baby hooters," as she called the owlets. She called them this because of the sound adult screech-owls make: *Hoot, hoot!*

The hungry owlets snatched the meat from the tweezers and swallowed the

Did You Know?

Different kinds of owls make different noises. Owls can purr, chirp, bark, whistle, screech, whinny, and—of course—hoot.

chunks whole. When their bellies were full, they tucked their heads into their feathers and fell asleep.

But soon, the babies lifted their beaks

into the air again. *Peep, peep!* they cried, begging for more food. All through the night, Mrs. Kuhn fed the baby hooters. She gave them water through an eyedropper, too. Eat, drink, sleep. Eat, drink, sleep. It went on like this for two days.

What Mrs. Kuhn didn't know is that owls need to eat bones, hair, and feathers, too. In the wild, the owlets' parents would have fed them the entire animal. Bones and hair help owls cough up pellets. Pellets are hard lumps the size of peanuts. They are full of the things that owls cannot digest. If owls don't cough up pellets every day, they can get sick. The baby hooters were not coughing up new pellets. Soon they lost energy. If Mrs. Kuhn did not find the owlets help soon, they would surely die.

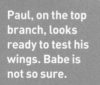

Paul, on the top branch, looks ready to test his wings. Babe is not so sure.

Chapter 2

RAPTOR RESCUE

Finally, Mrs. Kuhn had an idea. She called the Maryland Department of Natural Resources, or DNR. They knew someone who could help! The next morning, Mrs. Kuhn drove the owlets to the DNR. Workers there helped get the babies to the Owl Moon Raptor Center in Boyds, Maryland, U.S.A. Raptors are birds of prey, such as eagles, hawks, and owls. They use their hooked beak and sharp talons (sounds like TAL-uns), or claws, to hunt other animals for food.

Suzanne Shoemaker runs Owl Moon out of her home. Her house sits in a patch of wooded land. Blue herons, ducks, and beavers live around a stream winding through the woods. Foxes slink across the grass.

Suzanne is a wildlife rehabilitator (sounds like ree-uh-BILL-uh-tay-ter). She has a special permit to care for hurt and orphaned raptors. She opened Owl Moon in 2002. She built two outdoor flight cages, called mews (sounds like MYOOZ), for the raptors. Once the birds are healthy, Suzanne keeps them in the mews until they are strong enough to be released back into the wild.

Suzanne turned one room of her basement into an indoor mew. She covered the windows with netting, so the birds could not fly into the glass or out an open window. And she put tree branches around the room to give the birds a natural place to perch, or stand. Suzanne wanted the mew to feel like the birds' wild home.

Two adult screech-owls live in the indoor mew: Root'n Toot'n, a female, and Henry, a male. They play an important role at Owl Moon. They act as foster parents to baby owls that come to the center. Soon Root'n Toot'n and Henry would meet the new owlets. First, Suzanne needed to get the babies healthy.

As soon as the owlets arrived, Suzanne carried them down to the basement.

She placed the owlets on a table. Then she looked them over from beak to claw. The owlets were a healthy weight. But something was wrong.

The babies had not coughed up pellets in two days. They had no energy, and they were dehydrated (sounds like dee-HYE-drate-id). This means that their bodies weren't getting enough water. "Tammi Kuhn did the best she could caring for the owlets," said Suzanne. "But they weren't getting a good diet." Now it was up to Suzanne to save them.

Suzanne sprang into action. She used a syringe (sounds like suh-RINJ) to inject fluid under the owlets' skin. The fluid was like a clear sports drink for birds. This helped rehydrate them.

Next, Suzanne cut a dead mouse into small chunks. Suzanne calls this tasty bird treat "mouse mush." It includes the meat, the bones, and the organs, too. The bones would help the owlets cough up pellets.

Suzanne fed the babies mouse mush, using hemostats (sounds like HEE-muh-stats). Hemostats look like a pair of long, dull scissors.

Did You Know?

An eastern screech-owl can swallow a whole mouse in one gulp.

Finally, Suzanne put the babies inside an incubator (sounds like ING-kyuh-bay-tur). An incubator is a clear box. A fan pushes warm air inside the box. "At this point, the owlets needed to be kept warm, given fluids, and fed a proper diet," Suzanne said.

Raising Raptors

Raising baby raptors is hard work. If you want to release them, it is important that the birds do not imprint on, or become attached to, humans. If a wild raptor thinks humans are friendly, it might try to approach them. This would put the bird and humans in danger. Imagine if a hawk crashed your picnic! To make sure the owlets did not imprint on her, Suzanne wore a special outfit called a ghillie (sounds like GILL-ee) suit. It looks like it is made of leaves or moss. The suit covers the entire body. It camouflages (sounds like KAM-uh-flazh-es), or hides, a human's smell, too.

If Suzanne could get the owls healthy, she might be able to release them back into the wild. Over the years, Suzanne has cared for and released more than 500 birds. Normally, she re-nests owlets. She looks for a wild screech-owl nest with one or two babies inside it. She puts the orphaned owlet in the nest with them. Then she watches to see if the parent owls will adopt the new baby. Usually they do. If she can't find a wild nest, Suzanne puts the baby owls inside a birdhouse. Then she places the birdhouse high up in a tree near other wild owls.

"I try to get them into a situation where they can be raised by wild birds," says Suzanne, "even if they can't go back to their parents." If the babies could grow up around other owls, they could learn how to hunt on their own.

Over the next few days, Suzanne watched the babies closely. She fed them and gave them fluids three times a day. Soon, Suzanne's hard work paid off. The babies began coughing up pellets again. Their energy increased. It looked like the owlets would live!

Suzanne named the male owlet Paul, after a folktale character named Paul Bunyan. He was a giant lumberjack. Suzanne named the female Babe, after Paul Bunyan's buddy, Babe the Blue Ox.

A few days later, Paul and Babe opened their big, yellow eyes. Blink, blink. They looked up at Suzanne. Soon she would introduce them to Root'n Toot'n and Henry. And just maybe, she thought, she could re-nest the birds in the woods with other owls. But before she could release them, the owlets had to pass a test.

In the wild, owls hunt for their food. Screech-owls use their eyes and ears to find and catch food. They snatch insects out of the air. Or they perch on a tree and wait for a mouse or chipmunk to wander by. Then they pounce! Without their eyesight, screech-owls cannot hunt.

Suzanne knew that Paul and Babe had taken a bad fall when they were only days old. When Homer Kuhn cut down their tree, it hit the ground hard. If the owlets bumped their heads, their vision could be harmed.

Can these babies see? Suzanne wondered.

Babe perches next to her new friend at a nature center. He has red feathers, just like Paul.

HOOT, HOOT, HOORAY!

To Suzanne, the owls' eyes looked healthy. But to be sure, she drove the owlets to Dr. Jennifer Hyman's office. Dr. Hyman is an eye doctor for animals. She has treated dogs, cats, horses, hamsters, turtles, snakes, dolphins, penguins—and raptors. Now she was going to examine Paul's and Babe's eyes.

One at a time, Suzanne scooped

the owlets into her hands. She held them still, while Dr. Hyman lifted a small microscope up to each eye. The tool Dr. Hyman used is the same type your eye doctor uses on you, only it's smaller. Dr. Hyman carefully checked the owls' eyes. They didn't look good.

Little white dots speckled the lenses (sounds like LENZ-ez) of Paul's eyes. The dots are called cataracts (sounds like KAT-uh-rakts). They look like tiny ice crystals. Cataracts make things look cloudy instead of clear. Cloudy vision would make it hard for Paul to hunt. But the news got worse.

Babe had cataracts in her lenses, too. Only hers covered a larger area. This was very bad news for the owlets. If their cataracts got worse, they would never survive in the wild. All Suzanne could do now was wait to see if the cataracts spread in the owlets' lenses.

Suzanne drove Paul and Babe back to Owl Moon. It was time for them to meet their foster parents, Henry and Root'n Toot'n. If there was still a chance that the babies could be released, Suzanne wanted them to know other owls. She put Paul and Babe in a large wooden crate. Then she set the crate on a table inside the mew with Henry and Root'n Toot'n.

Did You Know?

Owls have no eyelashes. Instead, they have special feathers around their eyes called filoplumes (sounds like FYE-lo-plooms).

Henry flew over. He perched on the edge of the owlets' crate and peered inside. Root'n Toot'n stood on a branch nearby.

She bobbed her head from side to side. Suzanne lifted the owlets out of the crate and placed them on a branch near Root'n Toot'n. She knew that Paul and Babe were in good hands, or claws, now.

Over the next couple of weeks, the babies grew bigger and stronger. They watched Root'n Toot'n and Henry hop from branch to branch and fly around the room. Finally, Paul mustered the courage to test his wings.

First, Paul hopped from one branch to another. Then, he flapped his wings and flew a couple of feet to another branch. Soon, he was flying around the room. Paul flew without fear.

Babe was not so lucky. She tried hopping from one branch to another, too.

Helping Fallen Birds

What should you do if you find a small bird lying on the ground? "Don't pick it up," says Suzanne Shoemaker. Sometimes a bird may look hurt, but it's not. Suzanne says to call a wildlife expert first. They can tell you what to do. "They may want to see it for themselves, too," Suzanne says. How do you find a wildlife expert? Start with the National Wildlife Rehabilitators Association. You can find a directory of local professionals on its website: nwrawildlife.org.

But the little owl often missed her mark. She looked like a gymnast wobbling on a balance beam. Sometimes she fell. She never got hurt, but mostly Babe decided to stay put. This was a bad sign. Suzanne feared that Babe could not see well.

A few more trips to Dr. Hyman's office told the truth. Babe's cataracts had spread. They now covered a large part of each lens. Babe could see a little, but Dr. Hyman was sure that the owl would never be able to survive in the wild. The news made Suzanne sad. But she didn't give up. She decided to find a "forever home" for the owlet—a place Babe could stay for the rest of her life.

Meanwhile, Paul got good news from Dr. Hyman. His cataracts had not spread. He could see well. This did not surprise Suzanne. Paul had become an excellent flier.

The next step for Paul was to take something called a live-prey test. Suzanne drove him to the Tri-State Bird Rescue and Research Center in Delaware, U.S.A. The people there put Paul inside a large flight cage. Then they released live mice into the cage. Paul swooped down and snatched one of the mice in his talons. Over the next three weeks, Paul caught many mice. He passed the test!

Four months after Paul arrived at Owl Moon, he was released back into the wild.

Did You Know?

Owls have a third, clear eyelid. It helps protect their eyes as they swoop through thick brush to find prey.

It was a happy day for Suzanne. Now, she needed to find Babe a new home. But would anyone want the little owl with bad eyesight?

The answer was yes! Billy Heinbuch (sounds like HINE-buck) runs the Caitlin Dunbar Nature Center in Ellicott City, Maryland, U.S.A. He has a permit to raise raptors there. Billy had a male eastern screech-owl at the center. He had been looking for another owl to keep him company. He offered to give Babe a forever home.

Now, Babe lives in a large outdoor mew. There are lots of perches for her to stand on. And there is a nest box for her to sleep in. She shares the space with the male screech-owl, named Pygwidgeon (sounds like PIG-wid-jun).

Today, Pygwidgeon and Babe are educational ambassadors (sounds like am-BASS-uh-ders). They help teach people who come to the nature center about owls. "Everybody loves the screech-owls, because they're so small and cute," Billy says.

Was it the fall that caused Babe's cataracts? No one will ever know. But she has settled into her life at the nature center. Over time, she has explored every inch of her new home. Knowing where things are gave Babe confidence to test her wings again. She has even learned to fly around the mew.

Now both Paul and Babe are flying high in their new homes!

Get in line! Keepers at the David Sheldrick Wildlife Trust in Kenya lead elephant orphans on their daily walk into the forest.

ZONGOLONI:
OPERATION
ELEPHANT
RESCUE!

A mother
elephant grazes
on grass while
her little calf
keeps close.

BRAVE Little Calf

September 22, 2013
Teita Estate, Kenya

A family of elephants stood among some trees. Using their long trunks, they stripped leaves and branches off the trees, then brought the food to their mouths.

Two men stood nearby, watching the elephants. They worked as scouts. Every day, they patrolled the thick bushland on the vast Teita (sounds like TAY-tuh) Estate in Kenya. This area of the estate was set aside for wildlife. The scouts' job was to keep the wildlife safe from poachers. Poachers sneak onto other people's land to hunt wild animals. This is a big problem in many countries in Africa, even though it is against the law.

The scouts looked for traps that poachers set. And they kept an eye out for hurt zebras, lions, and other wildlife. When the scouts spotted the elephant family, they could tell right away that something was wrong.

One of the elephants walked with a limp. The scouts called their boss, Jen Carr-Hartley. They told her about the injured animal. Jen raced out to see the elephant for herself. "The elephant limped badly," she said. "I knew right away it needed treatment." Jen and the scouts guessed that poachers had shot the animal.

Poachers hunt adult elephants for their ivory teeth, or tusks. Hunting an elephant for its tusks is against the law, but poachers do not care. They know that some people will pay a lot of money for tusks that can be carved into statues and jewelry. Then these items can be sold for even more money.

Jen called a vet to come help the elephant. But daylight was fading. The vet could not treat the elephant in the dark. They would have to wait until morning.

Did You Know?

Elephants use their tusks to dig up tasty tree roots and scrape bark from trees. They also use them to defend against enemies.

Do You Speak Elephant?

Elephants use sounds and body language to talk to one another. For example, an elephant will turn its body in one direction, then it will lift its front leg and make a rumbling sound. That means, "Let's go this way." Elephant calves shake their heads from side to side to say, "Come play with me." When an elephant nods its head up and down quickly, it is not saying yes. That means it's angry. And if it stands tall and spreads its ears wide, watch out. This means, "Don't mess with me!"

When the scouts tracked down the hurt elephant the next morning, she was alone in the bush with a young calf. The rest of the family was nowhere around. *It's a mother elephant,* the scouts thought. Now it was even more important that they help her, or the calf would lose its mother. The scouts called Jen. She arrived a short while later with Dr. Poghon (sounds like POG-on), the vet.

Dr. Poghon shot a dart of medicine into the injured elephant's side to make her sleepy. But as soon as the dart hit the elephant, she turned and ran deeper into the bush. The calf, a female, followed her. Jen and the others ran after the elephants. By the time they reached the animals, the mother elephant had dropped to her knees.

The frightened calf was running circles around her. Dr. Poghon darted the calf, too. The calf quickly grew sleepy and lay down next to her mother.

Then the team got to work. They found a large, lumpy scab on the elephant's shoulder. Dr. Poghon cut open the scab to clean the wound. A large glob of smelly pus and blood spilled out. Hidden under the scab was a perfectly round hole, where a bullet had entered the elephant's shoulder. Jen and the scouts had guessed right. Poachers *had* shot the mother elephant. She was lucky to have escaped.

Dr. Poghon gave the elephant medicine to help clear up the infection and take away any pain. But the infection was bad. The vet was not sure if the mother would live. He gave both elephants medicine to wake them up. Soon, the elephants rose to their feet. Then they chased the humans back through the bush to their cars!

Over the next few days, the scouts saw the mother and her calf several times. The mother was still limping. And there was no sign of the rest of the family. "The mother may have been too weak to keep up with them," Jen says. Elephants usually travel many miles a day to search for food.

Then the scouts lost sight of the elephants. The mother and calf had wandered onto a ranch next to the Teita Estate.

By the time the scouts found the elephants a few days later, the mother was lying on the ground. The scared calf was nudging her to get up, but the mother was too weak. She could no longer stand. She barely moved at all. The scouts could tell the mother would not live. This made them very sad.

The calf was weak now, too. The scouts knew the little elephant could not survive without her mother and the rest of her family. So they decided to help her. They called Jen Carr-Hartley's husband, Kevin. Kevin manages the ranch where the mother had collapsed. Kevin and Jen quickly called the experts at the Kenya Wildlife Service (KWS) and the David Sheldrick Wildlife Trust (DSWT). "Can you help?" they asked.

"Yes!" the wildlife experts said.

Soon, several men from the KWS and the DSWT arrived. They walked toward the calf and her mother. The calf mustered all her energy. She stood tall. She spread her ears wide and charged at the men. She did not know they had come to help. She was protecting her mother. When the calf became too exhausted to fight, the men lifted her into the back of a truck. They drove to a nearby airstrip. A plane met them there and took the calf to her new home: the elephant nursery at the David Sheldrick Wildlife Trust.

The little calf was lucky. She had been given a second chance at life—but she still had a long way to go.

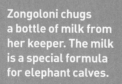

Zongoloni chugs a bottle of milk from her keeper. The milk is a special formula for elephant calves.

wore off, her mood changed. When she was wide-awake again, Zongoloni stood tall. She spread her ears wide, and she charged at the keepers. She seemed more scared than ever.

Zongoloni did not want anyone coming near her. "She was very aggressive and kept charging at the keepers," said Edwin Lusichi (sounds like loo-SEAT-chee), the head keeper. But that did not stop the keepers from trying to help the calf. They knew Zongoloni needed to eat if she was going to survive. So they placed a bucket of milk inside her pen.

The calf walked over to the bucket and put her trunk inside it. She slurped up all the milk. This was a good sign. If the keepers could get Zongoloni's body healthy, then they could work on making her happy again.

When Zongoloni was not charging at the keepers, she stood alone in her pen and hung her head low. These were signs that she was unhappy. Elephants become very sad when a family member dies.

Family is very important to an elephant. In the wild, elephants are born into large families, called herds. Herds are made up of mothers, daughters, sisters, aunts, female cousins, and young calves. Adult males live alone or with other males. Some elephant families have as many as 50 members!

The oldest and biggest female, called a matriarch (sounds like MAY-tree-ark), leads the family. She tells the others where to go and when to eat. But all of the older females work together to protect the young calves. The older females are called allomothers (sounds like AL-o-MUTH-ers). They're like babysitters. If a calf cries out, the allomothers rush to its side. They cuddle the calf with their trunks, and they rumble softly. It is like they are saying, "It's okay. We are here for you."

Family is important for other reasons, too. Elephants enjoy being around other elephants. And young calves love to play. They charge at other animals, such as warthogs, for fun. And they climb on top of the older elephants like human children climb on jungle gyms. To an elephant, family is everything.

The other orphans at the DSWT nursery had also lost their mothers and their families. They were very sad once, too. But over time they learned to trust the keepers. And they formed a new family.

At the DSWT, the keepers are like the matriarchs. They show the elephants where to go. They make sure they have enough food to eat. And the older orphans act like allomothers. They cuddle all the younger calves that come to the nursery. Could the other elephants convince Zongoloni to be part of their family?

Days passed. The keepers kept Zongoloni inside her pen. It would not be safe to let a charging, 900-pound (408-kg) calf run through the nursery. Or worse, the calf could run away.

Giant Bodies, Giant Hearts

Some scientists think that elephants have deep thoughts and feelings, just like people do. When an elephant dies, other members of its family hang their heads low and look sad. They form a line and walk by the body of their loved one, as if they are having a funeral. Sometimes, they even bury the body under tree branches. Months later the family returns to the body to visit the bones. They feel the bones with their trunks. They even pick them up and carry them around.

Did You Know?

In the wild, adult elephants form a circle around young calves to protect them from lurking predators.

At the nursery, there are pens for the elephants to sleep in at night to protect them from predators (sounds like PRED-uh-ters), such as lions and hyenas. But outside their pens, the elephants are free to roam—though they rarely leave their keepers' sides.

Every morning, the keepers would let the other elephants out of their pens. Then the elephants walked over to Zongoloni. They reached their trunks through the bars of her pen and cuddled her, like they do with all of the new elephants.

Then the keepers fed bottles of milk to the other elephants near Zongoloni's pen. Zongoloni watched the others gulp down their milk. She saw the keepers cuddle the calves. The elephants even sucked on the keepers' fingers. Every day, the other elephants formed a line and walked into the forest with the keepers. And every afternoon they returned, safe and sound.

Over time, Zongoloni stopped charging at the keepers. She even began to trust them. "She would approach the keepers for her milk and to suck their fingers," Edwin says. It seemed as though the other orphans had finally convinced the calf to join their herd!

Angela and Edwin agreed that Zongoloni was calm enough to be let out of her pen. But there was one more question to answer. Would Zongoloni stay with the other orphans? Or would she run away?

Older elephants at the DSWT welcome a young calf. The blanket helps keep the small calf warm on cool mornings.

Chapter 3

Finally, Zongoloni's big day arrived. The keepers opened her pen. They held their breath. Would she flee? To everyone's surprise, Zongoloni walked over to the other orphans. She took her bottle from a keeper. Then when the other elephants walked into the forest with the keepers, Zongoloni followed.

In the forest, the elephants looked for plants to eat. At noon, the keepers led the orphans to a water hole. The elephants splashed in the water and rolled in the mud. Then they vacuumed (sounds like VACK-yoomed) up dirt with their trunks and tossed it over their backs.

At first, Zongoloni stood off to the side a lot. This was a sign that she still missed her mother. New orphans often stand and eat alone. But over the next few weeks, Zongoloni warmed to her new family.

Soon, Zongoloni was splashing in the water and rolling in the mud with the others. She even made friends. She hung out with two of the older females, Quanza (sounds like KWAN-zuh) and Lima Lima (sounds like LEE-muh LEE-muh).

Sometimes Zongoloni got into mischief (sounds like MISS-chif). One day, she and

Lima Lima played hide-and-seek with a family of warthogs. The elephants trumpeted loudly. They chased the warthogs one way. Then the elephants turned and ran into the forest. Several minutes later, the elephants trumpeted again. The warthogs had found them! The elephants then chased the warthogs back through the forest.

Another time, Zongoloni and her pals played a game of "bush bashing." Bush bashing is when the elephants "push down shrubs and feel tough while doing it," says Angela.

Over the next few months, Zongoloni turned from a shy and lonely calf into a bold and confident one. When it was time to eat, she pushed the others out of the way. She wanted her bottle first.

Caring for Elephants

The David Sheldrick Wildlife Trust keepers work hard. They watch over the elephants all day and all night. Each evening, the keepers cover the baby elephants with blankets. Then they climb onto a bunk or curl up on a mat next to the calves. The keepers wake up every three hours to feed the calves bottles of milk. They love the elephants as much as they love their human families! You can read more stories about the elephant orphans—and rhino orphans, too—at sheldrickwildlifetrust.org/asp/orphans.asp.

"Zongoloni was—and still is—greedy with her milk," says Edwin.

One day, Zongoloni and Lima Lima decided they wanted more than their share of milk. They pushed over the wheelbarrow full of milk bottles. Bottles flew. Milk spilled. Then the two elephant pals shoved each other trying to get to the spilled milk!

Zongoloni could be naughty. But she could also be nice. A couple of months after she came to the David Sheldrick Wildlife Trust (DSWT), she began caring for the new baby elephants that came to the nursery. She cuddled them. She even let them suck on her ears.

Then Zongoloni really surprised the keepers. One day, a male calf named Faraja was sick. Zongoloni knew something was wrong. Faraja was usually playful. But that day he was quiet. He barely ate. Zongoloni stayed by his side all day. She cuddled him. Zongoloni, it seemed, had become an allomother.

By now, Zongoloni was more than two years old. Angela Sheldrick and the keepers decided that she was ready to take the next step toward being wild again.

In late June 2014, the keepers rounded up Zongoloni, Quanza, Lima Lima, and two more of the female calves. They drove them to Umani (sounds like OO-mon-EE) Springs, Kenya. The DSWT has a large fenced-in area there, called a stockade. It is surrounded by a forest.

When the orphans arrived at Umani Springs, they gulped down bottles of milk. They rolled around on the ground and sprayed dust on themselves. Then the keepers led the group into the forest. The elephants munched on plants, then splashed through a water hole. They seemed to love their new home.

That evening the keepers led the elephants back into the stockade. They closed the gate. When the sky turned dark, wild elephants approached the stockade. They rumbled at the calves on the other side of the gate. The orphans froze. Then they lifted their trunks into the air to smell the wild elephants. Zongoloni and the others didn't know it yet, but those elephants would soon become very important to them.

"Our orphans will make friends with the wild elephants," says Angela. The wild elephants will teach the orphans where to find food in the forest. They will take them to the best water holes. Most important, they will show the young elephants how to act and stay safe in the wild. These are lessons only other elephants can teach them.

One day, when the orphans get older, they will live with the wild elephants. But this step could take many years.

"Slowly, just as our own children do, they will stay out for a night with their friends," says Angela. If the orphans get scared during the night, a wild elephant will walk them back to the stockade. Then a keeper will open the gate to let them in. After one night out, the orphans will spend two, then three away from the stockade. In time, they will decide to be truly wild again.

But the orphans never forget their human family. Some return to the stockade to visit the keepers and to meet the new orphans. Some come back if they are hurt and need help. Others stop by just to play. And sometimes, an orphan will return with a big surprise: a calf of her own! Those are the best moments for the keepers and for Angela. It is when they know they have done their job well.

Everyone at the DSWT hopes to see Zongoloni with a calf of her own someday. Until then, they are happy knowing that she is well on her way to being wild again.

Heavenly the bear peers into the camera. The blue tag in his ear helps rescue workers identify him.

HEAVENLY: BRAVE BEAR!

A ski patrol member gives the young bear oxygen while they wait for the rest of the team to ski them down the mountain.

Mountaintop RESCUE

March 3, 2014
South Lake Tahoe, California,
U.S.A.

A small male black bear limped across the snow near a ski lift at Heavenly Mountain Resort. He stopped behind the ski lift shack and turned circles. Then the bear lay down. He tucked his cold, wet nose into his cinnamon-colored fur.

Joe Carmichael works at the ski resort. Every morning he goes up the mountain to check the ski lift, to make sure it is working okay. But this morning, a surprise was waiting for him. When Joe rounded the corner of the lift shack, he came face-to-face with the bear!

The bear popped his head up. Joe jumped back. "At first, it looked so small that I thought it was a coyote," Joe says. Slowly, Joe peered around the corner of the building again. Then he realized the animal was a bear. This surprised Joe. "It was odd to have a tiny bear out, especially at that time of year," he says.

It was still winter, the time of year when food is hard to find. Black bears around Lake Tahoe usually sleep through the winter, curled up in a den. The bears make their den in a sheltered spot, such as a cave, the inside of a hollow tree, or under a log. They stay there until spring arrives. Normally, the bears stay in their den until April. But it was only the beginning of March.

Why is this bear out of its den? Joe wondered. Could noisy skiers have roused (sounds like ROUZD) the bear from his sleep? Probably not. Had the bear woken up to take a midwinter stroll? Maybe. Bears sometimes do that. Or was it something else? Joe couldn't say for sure, but one thing was certain. Strange things had been happening in the Lake Tahoe area of California that year.

Spring had come early, and the weather

was unusually warm. Bears that lived at the bottom of the mountain were coming out of their dens earlier than normal. But high up on the mountain, the snow was still ten feet (3 m) deep. Most of the bears there were still fast asleep in their dens—but not this bear.

Joe tried scaring the bear back into the forest that surrounds the ski slopes. He grabbed two signs from inside the ski shack and clapped them together like cymbals. The bear didn't budge. "Go on, get!" Joe shouted. But the bear just stared at him. *Why isn't the bear moving?* Joe wondered.

Normally, black bears are afraid of humans. If a black bear sees a human, it should turn and walk the other way.

A Long Snooze

In early fall, black bears start getting ready for their long winter sleep. They eat lots of food to fatten themselves up. Then they find a sheltered spot to use as a den and line it with leaves, branches, and grasses. When winter comes, the bears curl up in their cozy dens and sleep, surviving on the body fat they built up over the summer and fall. When spring comes, the bears wake up and leave their dens. At first, they move slowly and don't eat much. But by summer, they are *hungry!*

But there was nothing normal about this bear. He just didn't care. Joe called his boss to report the animal. Skiers would be arriving soon, and a small bear would cause a stir on the slopes.

Joe's boss promised to send help soon. Meanwhile, Joe began checking the ski lift. He flipped a switch, and the chairs overhead roared into motion. A few minutes went by. Then the bear stood. He began walking up the mountain toward another ski slope. That's when Joe saw the blood. Bright red spots covered the snow where the bear had been lying.

Joe glanced at the bear. He saw a wound (sounds like WOOND) on the shoulder of his right front leg. He noticed that the bear limped when he walked, too. Joe reached for his phone. He called his boss again. "The bear is injured," Joe said. "He is going to need help."

Joe hung up the phone and walked out of the ski shack. He followed the bear up the slope. Then another strange thing happened. As soon as the bear saw Joe, he turned and walked back toward the ski shack. He turned circles in the snow and lay down again.

That's odd, Joe thought. He'd never had a bear follow *him* before. With the bear safely by the building, Joe stepped inside the ski lift shack to warm up for a few minutes. But as soon as Joe was out of the bear's sight, he rose to his feet. He started up the mountain again. Again, Joe followed the bear. And once again, as soon as the bear saw Joe, he returned to the ski shack and lay down.

"It was so strange," Joe says. "At the time, it seemed to me that the bear's mother wasn't there, so it was looking for somebody to take care of it." After that, Joe stayed outside. He didn't let the bear out of his sight.

A short while later, members of Heavenly Mountain Resort's ski patrol team arrived at the shack. They brought Carl Lackey, a local wildlife official, with them. Carl shot a dart full of medicine into the bear's leg. The medicine made the bear very sleepy. Then Carl pulled an oxygen mask over the bear's snout. Oxygen would help the bear breathe during the long, bumpy ride down the mountain.

Carl bundled the bear in a blanket and lifted him into a toboggan (sounds like tuh-BOG-un), a flat-bottomed sled. Then the Heavenly ski patrol skied the sled down the mountain to Carl's truck. Carl lifted the limp bear into the back of his truck and closed the latch tight. He drove off toward the Alpine Animal Hospital. He hoped doctors would be able to care for the injured bear.

Tom Millham
of Lake Tahoe
Wildlife Care
checks out
Heavenly's
hurt shoulder.

Chapter 2

TIME TO HEAL

On the way to the Alpine Animal Hospital, Carl stopped at Lake Tahoe Wildlife Care (LTWC). LTWC is a center that cares for injured and orphaned wildlife. It is run by Tom and Cheryl Millham. The Millhams agreed to care for the young bear while his wounds healed. They called the bear Heavenly. But first, Heavenly needed to see a doctor.

Tom climbed into Carl's truck, and they drove Heavenly to the animal hospital. Tom carried the bear inside and laid him on a metal table. Heavenly was still sleepy from the medicine Carl had given him on the mountain.

Kevin Willitts, a veterinarian (sounds like vet-er-uh-NAIR-ee-en), examined the bear from snout to paw. He felt all over the bear's body for bumps and scrapes. He opened the bear's mouth and looked at his teeth. He peered at his eyes, up his nose, and inside his ears. Then he x-rayed the bear's right front leg, the one with the wound over the shoulder.

The x-ray showed a small chip in Heavenly's bone. But Dr. Willitts wasn't worried. "It will probably heal on its own," he said. Aside from his injuries, the bear looked pretty healthy.

Dr. Willitts began cleaning Heavenly's wounds. The bear had a gash on his right shoulder. And he had two smaller cuts on his chest and back. The wounds had begun to scab over and heal. But they were infected.

Infected wounds can be painful. If left alone, they can also be deadly. Dr. Willitts shaved the fur around the wounds. He opened them up and cleaned them well. He told Tom the bear should feel better soon.

But how had the bear gotten hurt? Dr. Willitts couldn't tell. Maybe the bear had fallen out of a tree or down a hill. Maybe he tussled with another animal. Heavenly was only about a year old. Most bears that age would still have been with their mother.

Bear Care

Mother black bears give birth to one to four cubs in January or February. Newborn cubs weigh about 8 to 12 ounces (225 to 340 g). A mother bear keeps her cubs in the den until they are big enough to climb a tree. Climbing trees helps bears stay safe from enemies such as coyotes and wolves, which eat bear cubs. Most black bear cubs return to a den with their mother during their first full winter. By the next May or June, mothers force their year-old cubs to head out on their own.

Heavenly's mother would have kept her cub safe from predators. Coyotes and bigger bears kill young cubs. A mother would have taught Heavenly what to eat. She would have taught him how to forage (sounds like FOR-ij), or find food. But Heavenly was alone.

Where was Heavenly's mother? No one knew. That was another mystery. There were so many questions about the cinnamon-colored cub, but no answers.

"If only bears could talk," says Cheryl Millham. "That would make our job easier!" The important thing now, however, was that Heavenly was in good hands.

Dr. Willitts put a blue tag in Heavenly's left ear. It looked like a big blue earring.

It would help Tom and Cheryl tell Heavenly apart from the other bears at the center. Dr. Willitts wanted to see Heavenly again in ten days.

Tom drove Heavenly back to LTWC. He carried the bear into a large cage, called an enclosure (sounds like in-KLOH-zhur). Then he laid the bear on a blanket. There was a video camera inside the enclosure. It let Tom and Cheryl watch Heavenly from their computer. But the bear couldn't see them. That was important. If Heavenly got used to humans, he might try to approach them again in the wild. And the wild is exactly where Tom and Cheryl planned to put the bear. They just had to wait for his wounds to heal.

Tom and Cheryl have lots of experience caring for bears. Over the years, they have cared for 58 bears at LTWC. And they've released every one of them back into the wild.

When Heavenly's medicine wore off, he awoke to a feast. Cheryl had filled the room with lettuce, watermelons, and apples. Tom and Cheryl feed the bears at the center only food that is similar to what they would eat in the wild. The animals get no leftover food from Tom and Cheryl's meals. "Even though it would be a lot cheaper!" says Cheryl. Otherwise, when the bears return to the wild, they might follow their

Did You Know?

In the wild, black bears eat grasses, roots, berries, fruit, eggs, insects, fish, and other small animals.

noses. They might look for food in people's homes and trash cans.

Heavenly helped himself to the fresh fruit and vegetables. The bear ate until his belly was full. Over the next few days, Heavenly ate a lot. By the time his checkup rolled around ten days later, the bear had gained 24 pounds (11 kg)! He now weighed a whopping 73 pounds (33 kg). He had stopped limping. His wounds were healing nicely. Dr. Willitts cleared Heavenly for release into the wild.

Tom and Cheryl couldn't just release Heavenly anywhere, though. The California Department of Fish and Wildlife is in charge of finding new homes for rescued bears. The department decided it was not safe to put Heavenly back on the ski slope where Joe Carmichael had found him. Bears and skiers don't mix well. Heavenly would need to be released somewhere far away from ski slopes and houses. The people at California Fish and Wildlife started looking for the perfect place.

Meanwhile, at LTWC, Tom moved Heavenly into a bigger enclosure. The new space was like a playground for bears. It had logs to climb on and platforms to play on. Heavenly climbed and played. He swung on tire swings. He batted at balls that hung from the ceiling. Anyone watching the bear might have said that Heavenly was in heaven.

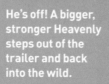
He's off! A bigger, stronger Heavenly steps out of the trailer and back into the wild.

Chapter 3

A Forever HOME

As the weeks passed, Heavenly grew stronger. Finally, California Fish and Wildlife found him a new home. It was in a large patch of forest. There were tall trees for Heavenly to climb. And there was plenty of food for the bear to eat.

The area was about 25 miles (40 km) away from the ski lift shack where Heavenly was found.

Three mountain peaks stood between the slopes at Heavenly Mountain Resort and Heavenly the bear's new home.

On April 23, 2014, Dr. Willitts arrived at Lake Tahoe Wildlife Care bright and early. He gave Heavenly medicine to make him sleepy again. Then he checked the bear's wounds. They were nearly healed.

Jason Holley, a biologist from California Fish and Wildlife, arrived. He loaded Heavenly into a trailer hitched to his pickup.

Jason climbed into his truck. His dog, Tasha, sat in the seat next to him. Jason patted Tasha on the head and drove off toward Heavenly's new home. Tom Millham and the LTWC team followed. Thirty minutes later they arrived at a clearing. By now the bear's medicine had worn off. Everyone gathered near the trailer to say goodbye.

Jason hopped out of his truck. He opened the trailer door. Heavenly stayed put. Jason banged on the side of the trailer. "Go on, bear! Go on!" he shouted. Heavenly lumbered out of the trailer. Then he stopped. He looked up at the humans.

"The bear seemed confused," Jason says. Most bears take off running. It was a good thing Jason had brought Tasha.

Tasha is a Karelian (sounds like kuh-REE-lee-un) bear dog, or KBD. KBDs are used to help scare bears away from humans. Jason kept Tasha on a leash but let her chase the bear. Tasha ran toward Heavenly. "Go on, bear!" Jason shouted.

Finally, the bear ran up a hill and climbed a tree.

Everyone agreed that Heavenly would be safe in the tree. They drove off. They were glad the bear was in the wild again.

But Heavenly's story doesn't end here.

Eight days later, Cheryl received a phone call. *Ring! Ring!* Someone had spotted a cinnamon-colored bear. It was digging through a trash can at a restaurant near Heavenly Mountain Resort. "Could it be Heavenly?" they wanted to know.

"No way," said Cheryl. The bear had been released only eight days earlier.

"He couldn't possibly have walked 25 miles (40 km) and crossed three mountain peaks in that time," Cheryl said. She thanked the caller and hung up the phone.

Did You Know?

Some bears that live near humans make their dens underneath people's houses.

The next day the phone rang again. *Ring! Ring!* This time, people had gotten closer to the bear. It had a blue tag in its left ear. Tom's and Cheryl's hearts sank. *How could it be?* they wondered. Of all the bears that Tom and Cheryl had released, none had returned. Why now? Why Heavenly?

Soon, other sightings were reported. Heavenly had been spotted in a nearby neighborhood. He lazed under pine trees in people's backyards. He sat on people's porches. He looked inside their windows. The bear was even seen walking across the roof of a home! The bear was fearless.

But why was Heavenly acting this way? Tom is pretty sure he knows the answer.

Keep Wildlife Wild

Heavenly's story teaches a very important lesson: Keep wildlife wild. If you live in a place where wildlife is common, make sure that your garbage is locked up. And don't leave pet food outdoors. Just visiting a wildlife area? Be sure to follow local rules when you get rid of your garbage. And never, ever feed wild animals. That can lead the animals to approach people.

"It's everyone's responsibility to help keep our wildlife wild," says wildlife biologist Jason Holley. That includes *you!*

"At some point before Heavenly's injury, he was probably fed by people in the area," says Tom. That's why the bear returned. That's why it showed no fear.

Other experts agree. "His mother probably taught him to find food near humans," says wildlife official Carl Lackey.

Most people who feed bears mean well. They think they are helping them. Other people forget to lock up their trash, and bears help themselves to the food scraps in it.

But feeding bears—on purpose or by accident—puts the animals in danger. They lose their fear of humans. And then they approach people. A small bear cub approaching humans may seem cute. But bears grow up fast. A 300-pound (136-kg) bear that approaches people is dangerous.

It was no longer safe for Heavenly to be in the wild. On May 5, Carl Lackey captured the bear again. He brought him back to LTWC. The best place for Heavenly now was in a sanctuary (sounds like SANGK-choo-er-ee). That's a place where humans could care for him.

Taking a year-old bear would be a big commitment. "Bears can live up to thirty years, and they cost around five hundred dollars a month to feed," says Nicole Carion. She works with the California Department of Fish and Wildlife. Growing bears also need a huge enclosure to live in. Finding Heavenly a new home wouldn't be easy.

Nicole made phone call after phone call. She spoke with the owners of several sanctuaries across the country. But nobody could take the bear. Weeks passed. Everyone was worried. What if they could not find Heavenly a new home? He couldn't stay at LTWC. There wasn't enough room.

Then, finally, some good news came. The Southwest Wildlife Conservation Center in Scottsdale, Arizona, U.S.A., said they would give Heavenly a new home. *Hooray!* Everyone cheered.

Southwest Wildlife is home to many rescued animals. Coyotes, bobcats, and mountain lions live there. Four black bears—Griz, Tahoe, Igasho, and Berry—live there, too.

On June 17, 2014, Heavenly was moved to Arizona. Today, he lives in his own outdoor enclosure at Southwest Wildlife. He sleeps in a cool den. He plays in his very own pool. He is even making new friends.

Heavenly shares a fence with Griz, Tahoe, and Igasho. The bears can see each other. Sometimes they touch noses through the fence. In a few months, when Heavenly is bigger, the director of the sanctuary plans to put him together with the other, older bears. In the meantime, Heavenly is enjoying his new home. The staff visits him every day. They bring the bear apples and grapes—his favorite treats. Heavenly, it seems, is in heaven again.

THE END

DON'T MISS!

NATIONAL GEOGRAPHIC KiDS **CHAPTERS**

KANGAROO TO THE RESCUE!

And More
True Stories of
Amazing
Animal Heroes

Moira Rose Donohue

**Turn the page
for a sneak preview . . .**

LULU: KANGAROO to the Rescue

Lulu takes a break from hopping to stretch out in the sun.

Lulu is happy to hang out with Luke Richards and his parents.

Chapter 1

Luke Richards and his friends were driving home late one evening.

"Watch out!" one of the boys yelled. "There's something in the road!"

Squee!! The driver hit the brakes and swerved. He avoided hitting the lump in the road.

"Pull over, mate," Luke said. He wanted to move whatever was in the road out of the way. Luke hopped out of the car.

The lump turned out to be a dead kangaroo. That would be a shock if you lived in the United States. But Luke lived in Australia. Millions of kangaroos live there, too. Unfortunately, sometimes they wander into the road in front of cars and trucks.

Luke was sad to see the kangaroo, but he knew he had to move it out of the way. He grabbed the animal by the tail and dragged it to the side of the road. It was heavy. Full-grown eastern gray kangaroos, or "roos," as they say in Australia, weigh about 145 pounds (66 kg).

Then Luke saw something amazing. The kangaroo's belly twitched. Kangaroos are a kind of mammal known as marsupials (sounds like mar-SOO-pee-ulz). Females have a pouch across their bellies. That's where they keep their babies, called joeys (sounds like JOE-eez). Luke put his hand in the pouch. Gently, he removed a joey. It had survived the accident!

Luke didn't think his parents would be happy if he brought the joey home. But he looked into the animal's frightened eyes. He just couldn't leave the little roo behind.

The joey was about the size of a cat. Luke wrapped it in his sweater. He climbed back into the car.

When he got home, Luke tiptoed into the house. He didn't want to wake his parents. He got some newspapers and covered

Did You Know?

When it's born, a baby kangaroo is hairless. It takes several months before its fur grows in.

the floor of his room. He offered the joey some water. Then he tucked the little roo snugly into his sweater. He draped the sweater over his bedpost. He hoped it would feel like the mother's pouch. Within minutes, both he and the joey were asleep.

The next morning, Luke's mother, Lynn, opened the door to his bedroom. It was a mess. She frowned. "Luke?" she called in a voice that said he was in trouble. Luke sat up. And like bread in a toaster, the joey popped up, too.

"I've got a little friend, Mum," said Luke.

"So I see," his mother sputtered.

Luke's family lived on a small farm. It was about 90 miles (145 km) west of the city of Melbourne. The farm was surrounded by land that was covered with wild plants and trees. This is known as "the bush" in Australia. Animals from the bush often wandered onto the farm. Sometimes Luke and his sister, Celeste, would find an injured one.

"They brought home a lot of king parrots that were hurt," said their father, Len. Once Luke and Celeste found a wounded opossum. They even rescued a wombat. They brought them to their father. He showed them how to nurse the animals.

But a baby kangaroo was another story. This joey was a female. She was about three months old. Normally, a joey doesn't even peek out of its pouch until it is four months old. At five or six months …

Want to know what happens next? Be sure to check out _Kangaroo to the Rescue!_ Available wherever books and ebooks are sold.

INDEX

Boldface indicates illustrations.

MORE INFORMATION

To find more information about the animal species featured in this book, check out these books and websites:

Face to Face With Elephants, by Beverly Joubert and Dereck Joubert, National Geographic, 2008.

National Geographic Animal Encyclopedia, by Lucy Spellman, 2012.

National Geographic Kids Mission: Elephant Rescue, by Ashlee Brown Blewett, 2014.

Wild Orphans, by Gerry Ellis, Welcome Books, 2002.

Owl Moon Raptor Center
owlmoon.org

Lake Tahoe Wildlife Care
www.ltwc.org

David Sheldrick Wildlife Trust
www.sheldrickwildlifetrust.org

Elephant Voices
www.elephantvoices.org

The Cornell Lab of Ornithology, All About Birds: Eastern Screech-owl
www.allaboutbirds.org/guide/eastern_screech-owl/id

North American Bear Center
www.bear.org

AUTHOR'S NOTE

I first heard about Heavenly's story from Tom and Cheryl Millham. The bear had arrived at LTWC only three weeks earlier. The National Geographic Kids Books staff and I lived the ups and downs of Heavenly's story in real time. We became so attached to his story that we even tried to help find the bear a forever home and get him there. In the end, the good folks at LTWC, California Fish and Wildlife, the BEAR League, and the Southwest Wildlife Conservation Center came together and pulled it off. When we heard the good news, we all jumped with joy!

For all the good men and women who rescue
and care for injured and orphaned animals
—A. B. B.

CREDITS

Cover (CTR), Suzanne Shoemaker; Cover (BACKGROUND), © Bidouze
Stéphane/Dreamstime, 4–5, Suzanne Shoemaker; 6, Suzanne Shoemaker;
11, © Eric Baccega/Nature Picture Library; 16, Suzanne Shoemaker; 22, Jan
Lewandrowski; 26, Phil Walker; 31, © Fergus Gill/2020Vision/Nature Picture
Library; 36–37, © Lisa Hoffner/Nature Picture Library; 38, © Robert
HENNO/Alamy; 42, © AfriPics.com/Alamy; 48, David Sheldrick Wildlife
Trust; 55, © Images of Africa Photobank/Alamy; 58, © Gerry Ellis/Minden
Pictures; 62, © Gerry Ellis/Minden Pictures; 68–69, Southwest Wildlife
Conservation Center; 70, Heavenly Mountain Resort; 75, barrett Hedges/
National Geographic Creative; 80, © 2014 Jak Wonderly; 84, © All Canada
Photos/Alamy; 90, © 2014 Jak Wonderly; 96, Daisy Gilardin/Getty Images; 101,
Bill Bachman; 102–103, Bill Bachman 104, AP Photo/Richards Family, HO; 111,
Suzanne Shoemaker

ACKNOWLEDGMENTS

Thank you to the following people for graciously sharing their time,
stories, and expertise with me:

Ann Bryant; Nicole Carion; Joe Carmichael; Caroline Blizzard;
Jen and Kevin Carr-Hartley; Chris Grasso; Sally Gunter; Billy
Heinbuch; Jason Holley; Dr. Jennifer Hyman; Liesl Kenney;
Tammi, Gary, Homer, and Willie Kuhn; Carl Lackey; Edwin Lusichi;
Sarah Milbourne; Tom and Cheryl Millham; Joyce Poole; Linda
Searles; Angela Sheldrick; Lina Sideras; Suzanne Shoemaker;
Kris Wheaton; and Dr. Kevin Willitts.

Thanks also to Scott Elder, whose *National Geographic Kids* article,
"Mission Animal Rescue: Elephant," was my first introduction to
Zongoloni. And a special thank you to Marfé Ferguson Delano,
Shelby Alinsky, and Jay Sumner from National Geographic.